MEDUSA

MONSTERS OF MYTHOLOGY

25 VOLUMES

Hellenic

Amycus
Anteus
The Calydonian Boar
Cerberus
Chimaera
The Cyclopes
The Dragon of Beotia
The Furies
Geryon
Harpalyce
Hecate
The Hydra
Ladon
Medusa
The Minotaur
The Nemean Lion
Procrustes
Scylla and Charybdis
The Sirens
The Spear-birds
The Sphinx

Norse

Fafnir
Fenris

Celtic

Drabne of Dole
Pig's Ploughman

MONSTERS OF MYTHOLOGY

MEDUSA

Bernard Evslin

CHELSEA HOUSE PUBLISHERS

New York   New Haven   Philadelphia

1987

EDITOR
Jennifer Caldwell

ART DIRECTOR
Giannella Garrett

PICTURE RESEARCHER
Susan Quist

DESIGNERS
Carol McDougall, Noreen Lamb

CREATIVE DIRECTOR
Harold Steinberg

Chelsea

First Printing

Library of Congress Cataloging-in-Publication Data

Evslin, Bernard.
Medusa.

(Monsters of mythology; bk. 3)
Summary: Recounts the story of the serpent-haired creature
whose gaze turned people to stone, and the adventures
of the hero who eventually vanquished her.
1. Medusa (Greek mythology) — Juvenile literature.
[1. Medusa (Greek mythology) 2. Perseus (Greek
mythology) 3. Mythology, Greek] I. Title. II. Series:
Evslin, Bernard. Monsters of mythology; bk. 3.
BL820.M38E97   1987   398'.45   86-28374
ISBN 1-55546-238-3

Printed in Singapore

For my granddaughter
KELLY EVANS
whose eyes once turned a stony heart
into enamored mush.

Characters

Monsters

Ceto (SEE toh)	Matriarch of the First Family of Monsters; half woman, half serpent; wife of Phorcys and mother of Echidne, Ladon, the Gray Ones, the Gorgons, Medusa, and several other litters of fearsome creatures
Phorcys (FOR sihs)	The Sea Hog; husband of Ceto and father to all of the above
Echidne (ee KID neh)	Eldest daughter of Ceto and Phorcys; also part woman, part serpent, but worse all around than her mother
Ladon (LAY duhn)	Totally serpent, and entirely lethal
The Gray Ones	Three hags, born old and growing steadily older, who must share a single tooth and eye amongst them and do so most unwillingly
Medusa (muh DOO suh)	Youngest of the Ceto-Phorcys brood; as beautiful as the others are ugly, and cursed for her beauty
The Gorgons (GOR guhnz)	Hideous elder sisters of Medusa, equipped with brass wings and brass claws
Andromeda's Beast	Sea dragon sent by Poseidon to harass the seaport city of Joppa

Gods

Zeus
(ZOOS)

King of the Gods

Poseidon
(poh SY duhn)

Brother of Zeus; God of the Sea

Athena
(uh THEE nuh)

Daughter of Zeus; Goddess of Wisdom

Hera
(HEE ruh)

Sister and wife of Zeus; Queen of the Gods; her jealous wrath carries its own legend

Humans

Danae
(DAN ay ee)

Princess of Argos; loved by Zeus and hated by her father, Acrisius

Perseus
(PUR see uhs)

Son of Zeus and Danae; young hero who meets many monsters in his quest for rightful succession to King Polydectes' throne

Acrisius
(uh KRIS ee uhs)

Cowardly king of Argos; father of Danae

Polydectes
(pahl ih DEHK teez)

King of Seriphus; pursuer of Danae

Cepheus
(SEF ee uhs)

King of Joppa; father of Andromeda

Andromeda
(an DRAHM ee duh)

Princess of Joppa; betrothed to Perseus; later queen of Argos, Mycenae, Seriphus, and Joppa

Others

Proteus
(PRO tee uhs)

Poseidon's aide; a minor sea-deity who changes shape at will

Dimona
(DEE mon uh)

Meadow nymph talented as a dream tinker

Atlas	The Titan condemned to bear the sky upon his shoulders
Apple Nymphs	Daughters of Atlas; also known as the Hesperides; three beautiful dryads who tend a perilous orchard
Chrysaeor (kry SAY or)	A handsome warrior born from the body of the beheaded Medusa
Pegasus (PEG a suhs)	The magnificent winged horse born from the body of the beheaded Medusa

Contents

1

A Fearsome Brood

This story begins in the sea and returns to the sea, but strange and terrible things happen in between.

In those first days there was no land, only water, until the gods grew bored with endless ocean and floated a few islands. A certain deep-dwelling family of monsters were happy to see these dry places heaving out of the sea. They knew that land would mean land animals, and they were tired of eating fish. The reason they had to live underwater is that they were so ugly the gods couldn't bear to look at them.

They hated the gods and vowed vengeance upon them— also upon a new species the gods were breeding for their entertainment, to be called humans.

The mother monster was named Ceto. She was half beast and half woman, with the body of a gigantic snake and the arms and breasts of a woman.

Her husband was Phorcys, the Sea Hog, a gross blob of flesh but much smaller than Ceto, who allowed him little freedom. She kept him wrapped in her coils except when she was laying her eggs.

These eggs hatched in strange ways.

Echidne crawled out of the first one. She lengthened into a woman-serpent like her mother but larger and of a much more ferocious nature.

Out of the second egg wriggled Ladon. He was pure serpent, a hundred feet long and every inch fatal. Half his length was jaw: fifty feet of living gullet lined with teeth. When the islands appeared, he crawled up out of the sea to hunt and could devour a hippo in two bites. An elephant took three.

The next egg cracked to reveal a set of triplets. At the sight of them, no one rejoiced. For they were born old: three crones with decaying hair and withered skin. They were blind and toothless most of the time, for they possessed but one eye and one tooth among them. These they had to share, passing them about to take turns seeing and chewing and always railing at one another for taking too long. The Gray Ones they were called, and Ceto couldn't wait to get rid of them. She carried them northward, swimming through water that grew colder and colder. Finally, she deposited them on an ice floe and swam away, never looking back.

Ceto laid two more eggs. The larger one was colored the usual leaden green to make it almost invisible underwater and more likely to escape the attention of a hungry neighbor. But the other egg, the smaller one, was a wonderful greenish gold, the color of the sea when the day dawns fair.

Now, Ceto and Phorcys had produced one ghastly offspring after the other and had no high expectations this time. But when the larger egg hatched, Ceto gasped in horror. Out crawled two scaly creatures with the bodies of infant girls. But they had brass wings and claws and were covered with brass scales. And their faces! Squashed noses, jutting fangs, and bulging red eyes. Their hair was seaweed.

"They're uglier than the Gray Ones," muttered their mother. "I'll take them to the ends of the earth and leave them there—and hope they don't fly back."

The lovely girl . . . didn't stay underwater, of course. She craved sunlight.

Finally, the smaller egg cracked. Out crawled the third sister. Again Ceto gasped, but in wonder. For this daughter was beautiful.

Monsters have no childhood. They grow up as soon as they leave the egg. So Ceto sat coiled in her undersea cavern, gazing upon her three tall daughters. "I can't exile these ugly ones," she muttered. The ancient Greek word for ugly one is *Gorgon*. "They must stay here and guard their sister. For anyone who sees her will want to abduct her immediately. Her name shall be *Medusa*, the lovely creature."

"Medusa?" grunted Phorcys, who spoke only once every hundred years; the rest of the time he was busy eating. "Why Medusa? The word means 'wise,' not 'beautiful.' "

"Quiet, Hog," said Ceto. "Or I'll squeeze you to a pulp. What is beauty but the body's intelligence?"

Indeed, the lovely girl who had been sent by fate to live among this monster brood lit up the undersea cavern, startling the shadows. She didn't stay underwater, of course. She craved sunlight and demanded that her sisters fly her as high as they could. They cleaved the air, swinging Medusa between them. Wingless though she was, she wanted very much to fly and made them drop her from great heights. She would straighten into a dive, hair streaming, and knife the water, then swim so swiftly that her sisters could not outrace her, no matter how fast they flew.

2

The Necklace

A rumor arose that Poseidon was about to choose a bride. For some reason gossip spreads just as fast underwater as it does above. Immediately, every Nereid in the Ocean Stream, every river nymph, and every naiad of fountain and lake swam into the Middle Sea. There they hovered in shoals about his great sunken palace of coral and pearl. Wherever Poseidon went he found them swarming, darting in and out of his path, brushing against him, tweaking his beard, and calling to him in the curious bubble language of the submerged.

"I'd better do something drastic," he muttered. "Or they'll wear me down by sheer weight of numbers. I have a great deal of endurance, but I can't handle them all."

Poseidon thought and thought and finally hit on a plan. He summoned his chief helper, a watery demigod named Proteus, who was gifted with the ability to change his shape. He could become jellyfish, octopus, shark, abalone—whatever the occasion required, and all in the wink of an eye. But his favorite guise was that of a blue-eyed white seal, and it was in this form that he now appeared to Poseidon.

"You called me, oh master, and I am here."

"Yes, faithful Proteus. I have need of your services."

"Command, and I perform."

"As you know, I am about to take a bride," said Poseidon. "Every nymph and naiad and Nereid from every waterway of the world seems to be competing for the honor. And they are all so bewilderingly beautiful that I simply cannot choose among them."

"A pleasant dilemma, my lord."

"What I want you to do is organize a swimming race."

"They all swim superbly, your majesty."

"Some have to be better than others, and among those, one has to be the best. It is the nature of things; there is always one who's best."

"Shall I announce that you will marry the winner?"

"No, no . . . we must still leave ourselves some options. Announce that they will be racing for a prize, a jewel most sumptuous, the exact nature of which we shall not disclose until after the race."

"Yes, sire. They swim. One of them wins. Then what?"

"I shall have been closely observing the swimmers, judging them on strength, speed, endurance, and so on—qualities any wife of mine will need in full measure. Among the ten or so who come in first will undoubtedly be some magnificent creatures. I shall choose among the finalists."

"All will be done according to your pleasure, my lord."

The white seal who was Proteus swam away, changing himself into a shark as he went—for that is the species best suited for organizing contests.

Thereupon, Poseidon sent for Brontes, a Cyclops, who had won the sea god's admiration by hammering out a set of enormous silver horse troughs for his herd of surf-stallions.

"I have a task worthy of your skill, Brontes. I want you to make me a gem that I will be proud to offer my bride. It must be a necklace, the most magnificent ever seen or imagined in

Wherever Poseidon went he found them swarming,
darting in and out of his path, brushing against him . . .
calling to him.

heaven, on earth, or under the sea. You shall have an entire harvest
of pearls—black ones and white ones, brimming with watery
lights and filtered moon fire. You shall also have a sunken galleon
whose hold is loaded with treasure. From its heaviest ingots you
shall forge a golden chain to hang the pearls on. And of the
diamonds from the galleon, you shall select the largest, the most
brilliant and artfully cut, to stud the boundaries between white
pearls and black."

"How splendid!" cried Brontes. "How generous! All the goddesses will go mad with jealousy."

"Yes," said Poseidon. "And my bride, lucky creature, noting their envy, will go mad with joy, which is as it should be. Hasten your labors, good Brontes. I give you ten days."

"On a task like this, sire, I shall work both day and night."

Athena was silent. She kept staring
at the necklace, naked desire in her gray eyes.

Before Brontes could finish his assignment, however, he was visited by Athena, Goddess of Wisdom, the warrior maiden whose tactical skills rivaled those of her half brother, Ares, Lord of Battle. She had come to order weapons—a new-moon sword, a dagger, and a set of spearheads. Brontes was working on the necklace as she entered. Athena moaned with pleasure when she saw what lay on the basalt slab that was his workbench. It seemed as though the forge fire had burst, scattering varicolored coals upon the slab.

"What are you making?" she whispered.

"A necklace, my lady."

"May I know for whom?"

"For whomever Poseidon chooses."

Athena was silent. She kept staring at the necklace, naked desire in her gray eyes. She coveted this gorgeous jewel with a craving that scorched her inside, and she was resolved to have it for herself, come what might.

3

Family Council

he Middle Sea was boiling with excitement as the day of the great race approached. The most excited of all, perhaps, was Ceto. Beyond anything else in the world she wanted her beautiful daughter to become Poseidon's bride. She called the Gorgon sisters to her and said:

"Which of you is which?"

"Why the sudden interest, mother?" said one. "Considering that you've never even bothered to name us."

"Well, you've named yourselves, haven't you?" Ceto replied. "Don't be impudent, my lass, or I'll mangle you, brass scales and all. Which one are you?"

"I am Strong," muttered one Gorgon.

"And I am Swift," said the other.

"Strong and Swift," said Ceto. "Well, you are, you are. Ugly as the hinges of hell, but strong and swift, no doubt about that. And I want you to use your strength and speed to help your sister."

"Help her do what?" said Swift.

"We're always doing things for her," said Strong. "She's been queening it over us since we were born. I suppose that's all right. We don't have anything better to do than fly her around and guard her against kidnappers and so forth. But I wouldn't say she needed anybody's help, not little sister Medusa. She takes excellent care of herself."

"Shut your spiteful mouth!" shouted Ceto. "I must know this: Is she fast enough to win Poseidon's race?"

"She's fast enough," said Swift. "She can swim circles around anything in the sea."

"She can, but will she?" asked Strong.

"What do you mean?" said Ceto.

"Medusa forgets what she's doing. She starts dreaming. If she even remembers to enter the race, she'll take the lead easily—then she'll see a pretty piece of coral or fall into conversation with an octopus. Everyone will swim past her and she won't even notice."

"Suppose I swim with her and keep nagging her back on course?" said Ceto.

"Well," said Swift. "It might work for a while, but if she gets interested in something else, she'll simply swim away. You won't be able to catch her."

"I can catch up with her while she's looking at the coral or chatting with the octopus."

"In the meantime," said Swift, "the race will be over."

"All right," said Ceto. "We have to do two things. I have to swim with her and keep her in the race. And, what you two must do is interfere with the other swimmers."

"How?" said Strong.

"What happens when a gull swoops down on a school of fish?"

"They scatter. They go deep."

"Well . . . you two will be my gulls. Or sea hawks is more like it. You will fly over the course, and when you see naiads, Nereids, and other nymphs beneath you, you will plunge through the air, claws gleaming, screeching. Like frightened fish, the swimmers will scatter, dive, and hide in the depths. Then you two will circle above, clashing your brass wings, rattling your brass claws, screeching, and shrieking until I can get your sister on the move again."

"It'll be a slow race," said Swift.

"But she'll win, she'll win. She'll be Poseidon's bride, and Queen of the Sea."

"Do you really want her to marry that brawling bully? He'll make a dreadful husband."

"He'll also make her a queen," Ceto said. "Afterward, she can ignore him through eternity."

"Yes . . .," said Strong. "She might not even notice she's married. She'll sit on a rock winding the necklace in her hair, admiring herself in the mirror of the sea, and won't give Poseidon a thought."

"He'll be marrying better than his brothers did," said Ceto. "Zeus has Hera, the shrew of the universe. Hades abducted Persephone and has been hated by her for a thousand years now. If my beautiful girl grants Poseidon one smile, he'll be doing better than his hag-ridden brothers. Off with you now! Go practice dropping out of the sky, shrieking as you go. Find a school of dolphins and practice on them. Who knows—you too may profit from your sister's success. She may be able to find husbands for you."

"Will she be that powerful?" muttered Swift.

"I suppose anything's possible," said Strong. "After all, mother, you found a husband, and you're no beauty. It was only *him*, of course." She pointed a claw at Phorcys, who lay snoring within Ceto's coils. "But we'd settle for anything, wouldn't we, sister?"

"Even less," said Swift.

They flew off, shrieking with laughter.

4

Bride of the Sea

edusa sat on a rock, plaiting her hair and singing. Her voice harvested the sounds of the sea—gull cry, splash, and sigh; lilt of water and lament of wind; chuckles of the tide among pebbles; and the moon-drunk crooning of naiads catching fishermen. As she sang, she combed the mass of hair. Each strand was a tendril of light, a filament of fire. These rich tresses, trapping the sunshine all day, held it at night and became a false beacon to helmsmen, luring them out of darkness to break their ships upon the rocks. All this she made happen as innocently as a child whipping the heads off flowers. Shipwreck was her pastime; her voice called sailors to drown.

One night, riding in his dolphin chariot, Poseidon heard a voice singing. Although he was as tone-deaf as a mackerel, he knew that this voice could belong only to someone beautiful. Surfacing, he saw Medusa plaiting her hair; it was a net of moonlight, casting a fragrance of wild grasses upon the salty wind.

The night was cool, but the sea around him began to steam with his desire. He knew that he had found his bride, and tried to tell her so, but could not utter a word. His desperate craving had wiped his lips of speech. He roared wordlessly.

Medusa on her rock looked up to see a huge, green-robed, green-bearded figure balancing himself on the swell. Dolphins frisked about him. He held an enormous three-pronged staff and wore a crown of pearls. He bellowed again and brandished his trident. She smiled at him. And he found speech.

"Who are you?" he said.

"Medusa."

"You shall be my queen."

"Are you king of something?" she asked.

"I am Poseidon."

"But Poseidon, I hear, has a wonderful gift for his bride."

"Here . . . "

He spun a hoop of fire toward her. She caught it on her arm. It was the necklace.

"If you take it you are my wife," he said.

"Yes, your majesty."

And so it was that Poseidon called off the great race, putting an end to every tender expectation. He had chosen his bride.

News of Medusa's triumph spread through the Middle Sea, enraging its nymphs. It became unsafe to put out in a small boat for fear that a Nereid would swim under it, capsize it, snatch a sailor, and carry him off to an undersea cave. There, she presented him with a choice: marry her, or be fed to the sharks.

Meanwhile, Medusa sat on her rock playing with her necklace, making its mingled lights flash back at the stars. A small boat scudded by, running before the wind. A fisher-lad had bound the rudder and was standing in the bow, arm raised, ready to cast his spear at one of the big sail-finned fish, which were not the best eating but were the easiest to catch.

He was a slender youth, just ripening into manhood. Standing there in the bow, spear poised, painted by moonlight, he seemed to be carved of marble. Medusa's heart danced at the sight of him.

The boat stopped suddenly, as if it had hit a rock. She stared

A small boat scudded by, running before the wind.

in disbelief; she knew there were no rocks around except the one she was sitting on; she thought the boat must have been gripped by an octopus. But it was no octopus. A Nereid surfaced, seized the lad by the hair, and pulled him under. Medusa dived off her rock. She reached the sea nymph in three strokes and took her by the throat. The Nereid writhed and flailed her legs, but Medusa

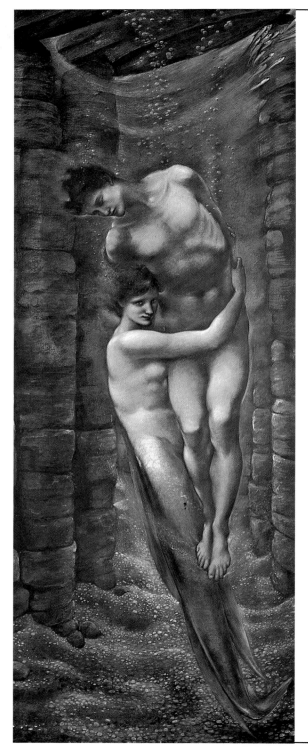

A Nereid surfaced,
seized the lad by the hair,
and pulled him under.

was much larger and stronger. She pulled the nymph to the surface—for you cannot strike hard underwater—and slapped her until she fled, weeping.

Medusa caught the boy, who was feebly struggling in the water. She set him astride her and swam on her back until she reached the rock. There, she lifted him out of the water and climbed onto the rock after him. His teeth were chattering and his lips were blue.

She took him on her lap and hugged him close, feeling the heat of her body enter his, and his shudders subsided. He looked at her and smiled faintly. A big purple bruise was forming on his brow. He closed his eyes. His head lolled against her shoulder. She held him as though he were a child, rocking him in her arms, crooning. Very gently, she kissed the side of his face. His eyes opened. He smiled.

Suddenly, the stars were blotted. A cold wind blew. The sea churned. Medusa, startled out of her trance, lifted her face, tasting the wind with animal alertness. Had Poseidon spied them together on the rock and grown jealous? Sent a squall? Would it grow to the kind of killer storm that the sea god sent against those who offended him?

Quickly, she slid the boy off her lap. "Wait here," she said, and dived off. She cut through the water toward the drifting boat, caught its line, and towed it back to the rock. She motioned to the boy, who climbed down into the boat.

"Go!" she cried. "You must not stay here—not now!"

He gazed at her sorrowfully. A hot gust of tenderness swept over her. But she knew she must not yield to it; the peril was too great.

"Go now!" she cried. "Go, little love. Sail away."

"Must I?"

"Come tomorrow at sunset. Sail past the rock. If all is safe, I shall be singing. If I am silent, you must sail away."

The youth raised his sail; the boat moved into blackness.

5

The Curse

he tidings that had so aroused the sea nymphs reached Athena's mountaintop. Burning with envy, Athena whistled up her chariot, which was drawn by eight white arctic owls, as large as eagles. She flew off her mountain and skimmed the surface of the water, searching. Finally, she saw a patch of light fracturing, exploding into color. Making herself invisible, she hovered over Medusa's rock, watching her wind the necklace in her hair. Athena knew that she was gazing upon the most gorgeous creature in the entire world, and that knowledge clawed her entrails, gouged the soft places behind her eyes, and seared every particle of her body with jealousy.

"Very proud of yourself, aren't you," snarled Athena. "Well, take a last look. I'm going to make you even uglier than your sisters."

Medusa raised her comb and felt it snatched from her hand. She looked up, thinking a gull had seized it, but saw nothing. She stared then into the mirror of the sea, and her eyes grew stony with horror. A snake was coiled in her hair; it held her comb in its jaws. Shrieking, she reached up and grasped the snake, trying to pull it out of her hair, but its tail was rooted in her head; to pull it out she would have to rip away her scalp. And now the snake became two snakes, then three! Every lock of her hair was becoming a snake. They stood on their tails, weaving their coils, darting their tongues, hissing.

The sinking sun reddened the water. Medusa, staring at her reflection, saw the snakes writhing out of her head like flames. She could not bear the sight of herself. Red-hot pincers of grief were digging into her heart. But she did not know how to weep, for the tears of creatures that live underwater are lost in the sea. She heard herself howling. She lifted her face to the sky and howled like a wolf.

At that very moment, the fisher-lad she had saved was coming back to her. He yearned to be with her on the rock again and prayed that he would hear her voice, for she had said that if she were singing at sunset it would be safe for him to come. He heard her. He was so enamored of her voice that her wild cries of grief sounded like song.

She didn't see him. Sailing toward her out of the flaming disk of the sun, he was only a silhouette. He dropped sail, wedged his bow in a cleft of rock, and climbed up beside her.

"Medusa!" he cried.

And she, seeing him appear out of nowhere in the midst of her torment, hearing the love in his voice, lost all sense of everything except his return. She sprang up, lifted him to her, and tilted his face to kiss him. He stared at her, sinking into nightmare. Her beautiful, graceful head was crowned with snakes. They were her hair. Each one separately alive, they were the coiled shapes of evil. They were writhing, lunging, hissing. The horror entered him, freezing every response, petrifying every duct and fiber, damming the flow of blood.

Medusa felt him stiffen in her arms. His eyes grew rigid. The thread of vein at the base of his throat stopped pulsing. She was holding a stone boy. He slipped out of her arms, fell stiffly off the rock, and crashed into his moored boat, splintering it. Amid wrecked timbers, he sank out of sight.

The sinking sun reddened the water.
Medusa . . . saw the snakes writhing out of
her head like flames.

Medusa stared into the purple-red water. She stood there watching as if carved of marble herself, motionless except for the snakes swaying on her head.

"I'm the ugliest sister now," she cried to the wind, "the worst Gorgon there is. So horrible that anyone who looks upon me turns to stone. Yes-s-s . . . you came sailing back to me, little love. And saw a change so loathsome that your very heart froze. You're a marble boy now, sleeping whitely, heavily, at the bottom of the sea. Your bones will turn to coral, and your eyes into black pearls, more precious than those of this necklace, which is the sea god's accursed gift. As for me, I shall hide my ugliness

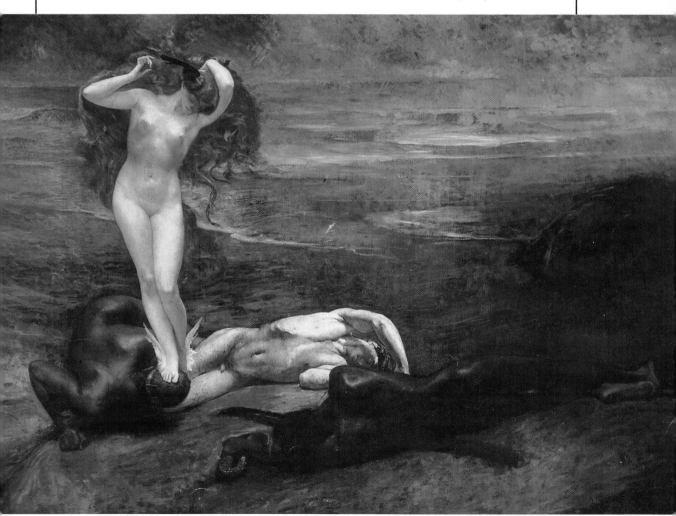

"I'm the ugliest sister now,
the worst Gorgon there is. So horrible that
anyone who looks upon me turns to stone."

where no one may ever set eyes upon it again. I shall swim to the end of the Ocean Stream to the region beyond the North Wind, where it is neither land nor water but foul, icy swamp, unvisited by sun or moon, shunned by fish, and avoided by birds. There shall I abide forever and ever, knowing the full torment of immortality—unwilling to live, unable to die."

Medusa threw her necklace away. But it never reached the water. The invisible Athena caught it in midair, whipped up her owls, and flew off toward her mountain, laughing triumphantly.

Swimming toward the lair of the North Wind, Medusa found bitter entertainment in turning sharks to stone. One day, however, a dolphin that had been her playmate spotted her. Before she could turn away he had become a stone dolphin and dropped to the bottom of the sea.

From then on, Medusa tried to avoid every living thing, but once, passing a headland, she entangled herself in a heavy net strung between two fishing boats and was hauled to the surface before she could break free. Shouting with joy at the weight of their catch, the fishermen pulled up the net and looked down on Medusa and the snakes that were her hair. They became statues, smiles carved upon their faces. They had died rejoicing.

After that, Medusa swam very fast and without rest. The exercise heated her blood, and, because she was still very young, she sometimes forgot the dreadful thing that had happened to her, and found herself filling with joy. Then she would feel the snakes tugging at her scalp, and remember what she had become. And grief revived was more agonizing than if it had never ceased.

6

Guests of the Tyrant

Polydectes, king of Seriphus, was famous for ferocity even among the cruel rulers of the Middle Sea basin. When enraged, he would kill anyone within reach. By the time he was thirty-seven he had run through three wives and had sent several children to join their mothers in Hades.

Now, he was considering a fourth wife. The target of his dangerous attentions was a beautiful young woman named Danae, who had come to Seriphus from a far place. Since her arrival she had wrapped herself in mystery, refusing to disclose her rank, her parentage, or the father of her son. Anyone looking at her, however, knew immediately that she had sprung from a line of conquerors, both male and female. In those days, women fought alongside their men when they didn't have more important things to do.

Danae had to be polite to the king, for she lived on Seriphus as his guest. But she secretly loathed him and was resolved that she would kill herself rather than become his wife. "But I shall not leave this life without a royal escort," she said to herself. "If I decide to travel to the Land Beyond Death, I shall play the role of loving bride and insist that my husband accompany me wherever I go."

Nevertheless, Danae was clever enough to conceal her feelings, and she managed to fend off the king without arousing his fury. But he was growing more ardent, and she knew she wouldn't be able to go on refusing him much longer.

Polydectes was not a stupid man, and although his mind was larded with the kind of vanity that often dulls the wit of tyrants, he realized that Danae was prepared to repulse him. He refused, however, to ascribe her lack of interest to his own lack of charm. He had to find someone else to blame and decided that it was her young son, Perseus, who was poisoning her mind against him. The king thereupon resolved to get rid of Perseus, but to do it in such a way that he would not be blamed for the boy's death.

Seriphus was an island whose chief industry was piracy. The most successful pirates became its first nobility; its first king had been a glorified pirate chief. Now, five generations later, king and nobility were still pirates, slightly polished. In such a society, the children tended to play roughly, and Perseus and his friends were the roughest of all; any game was likely to end in a brawl.

But Perseus in sport, as in everything, went further than anyone else. For him fighting was a natural extension of other games—the most exciting form of activity. And he fought with great playfulness and a mounting joy. At the height of a conflict he felt a kind of love for the antagonist who provided such sport. This lightheartedness translated itself into light-footedness. Where others grew grave with determination and heavy with rage, he shed gravity. Perseus moved more quickly, leaped higher, and struck so swiftly that his fists seemed to blur in the air. He kicked like a wild stallion, butted like a mountain goat. He used dagger and sword and spear as a tiger uses its claws, or a wild boar its tusks.

Upon a certain day, the king stood half hidden behind a rock watching the children play at the base of the hill. His heart grew bitter within him as he watched his young enemy move among the other boys like a hawk upon barnyard fowl. His hair burned yellow; his bronze body flashed; his eyes shot rays of light. And the king knew suddenly that the woman he loved and the boy he hated lived somewhere beyond ordinary circumstance; they were a different breed—more vibrant than life. To win the mother and vanquish the son, he would have to do things he had never done before.

He went to consult an oracle. It took two days and a night for the old prophet to search for clues to the king's future. On the first day he examined the entrails of a pigeon. On the second, he studied the flight of wild geese. And, on the night between, he stayed awake to read the stars.

By this time, Polydectes was boiling with impatience, and the oracle was afraid to take any more time. "Oh Majesty, forgive me," he said. "But the signs are difficult to read. The pigeon's liver was where its lungs should be, and its heart was riddled with worms. The stars were pulsing in a way I've never seen, spinning like fire wheels, branding the black sky with strange images—a nest of snakes, and statues, bleeding. As for the flying geese, they scrawled the sky in a language more ancient than our own, but I sensed their message—which is 'peril . . . peril . . . peril!' "

"What kind of peril?" asked the king.

"Obscure, sire. Ugly but obscure. What it reduces to is this: Your enemy is the son of a god and cannot be defeated by direct assault."

"Can he be defeated at all?"

"Only by deceit—by lies artfully told and plots skillfully spun."

Polydectes looked hard at the old man, who shuddered. He turned and departed; the prophet almost swooned with relief.

"The old dotard only advised me to do what I had already decided to do," thought the king. "But that's an oracle's stock in trade, it seems . . . especially when his client is a king. As for Perseus being the son of a god, that means that his mother was once loved by a god. And that means . . ." Polydectes smiled to himself, for it tickled his vanity to think of wooing the woman a god had loved; it seemed to make him something of a god himself. "As for weaving a plot to lead the lad to his own death, that suits me very well. I'll start with his mother."

Polydectes invited Danae to his palace.
They sat drinking wine on a balcony.

Polydectes invited Danae to his palace. They sat drinking wine on a balcony overlooking a great scoop of sea, painted by the sunset. He had subdued his ferocious manner for the occasion, smiling at her benevolently.

"Hear me, my dear," he said. "Though I am all-powerful here, I am ready to accept the fact that you do not return my love. Nevertheless, that love abides. What I must do is change its nature. I shall love you not like a husband, but like a brother . . . or like a father, perhaps."

"Please!" cried Danae. "Don't say 'like a father.' Don't say 'father' to me."

"Mystery within mystery!" cried Polydectes. "What do you mean?"

"I welcome your change of heart," said Danae. "And I shall gladly accept you as my brother."

"Then I claim a brother's due and would know the secret that you harbor."

"Ah, brother, it is a terrible tale I have to tell." For a moment, Danae hesitated. "My father was Acrisius, king of Argos. I was his only child. Although descended from mighty warriors, he was a coward. And I was causing him much terror. He knew I would soon be ripe for a husband, and that husband would be a prince or a young king—a warrior, certainly. My father visualized the son-in-law he did not have yet reaching for power in Argos, gathering troops, and plotting to murder him. It became unbearable for me to enter his presence; his eyes were glazed with hatred. Finally, a dreadful rumor reached my ears. My father had consulted an oracle, who had stoked his terror by telling him that if I bore a son, that son would kill him. Knowing my father, I decided to flee the palace, but it was too late. He forbade me to leave the royal enclosure and set guards upon me."

"How is it he didn't kill you immediately?" said Polydectes.

"He feared the vengeance of the gods. He had heard they inflict terrible punishment on those who kill their children."

"Sometimes yes, sometimes no," muttered Polydectes. "Go on."

"I had been hearing a daylong clanging of tools against metal, and I didn't dare think what that sound foretold. My father had ordered a prison built that would need no jailers—for he wanted to deprive me of male society forever. So his slaves were building a brass tower without doors or windows, just a single arrow slit for light and air. I was put into that tower before it was finished and watched the last plate of brass being bolted into place. There my father meant me to dwell until I died—which he expected to happen quickly. For I had always been an active girl who loved to ride and hunt and run on the hillside and swim in the sea."

"Poor child," murmured Polydectes. "Poor innocent wild-flower of a child with so cruel a father."

"So he waited for report of my death, and waited, and waited. . . . But I was resolved not to die." Danae broke off suddenly, stifling a sob, then said: "Dear brother, forgive me; I can't go on. What happened next in that tower is a holy secret to me; I have told no one, not even my son. And I'm still unwilling to talk about it."

"Don't fret. You'll tell me when you're ready. We shall have many such talks, my sister, and you will find yourself opening your heart to me."

"Yes . . . no doubt."

"And now," said Polydectes, "to show you how different I am from your cruel father, I shall designate your son to be my heir. Yes, he shall inherit the kingdom after my death. Nor do I fear that he will do anything to hasten that sad event, although many kings would be fearful, for he bids fair to develop into a powerful and ambitious young warrior."

Danae was truly surprised. "I don't know how to thank you," she murmured.

"I am not looking for gratitude. I am here to serve you in all ways without thought of repayment."

*"I knew he was a god. . . . Every night he came
into my cell as a shower of gold, and he vanished at dawn—
just like the evening star."*

"Your generosity overwhelms me, sire."

"I must add that my gift to Perseus, like most gifts, carries with it a certain obligation, not to me, personally, but to the state. According to our law, no one can inherit the throne without performing a deed recognized as heroic. I, myself, the son of a king, had to venture forth alone in a small boat to combat a killer whale that was harassing our coast. Armed only with a spear, I succeeded in killing the monster and thus qualified myself for the kingship. Your son will choose his own task."

"Let me go now, dear brother," said Danae, "and inform Perseus of your noble generosity."

That night, mother and son sat long over a driftwood fire as she told him what had happened that day. Perseus listened hungrily, growing more and more excited with each word.

"Mother, mother!" he cried. "What great warrior shall I challenge? What monster shall I hunt? Or shall I go to places no one has ever gone before? Sail to the very end of the world where the sea tumbles off into nothingness? Shall I lean over and peer into the abyss—or leap off, perhaps to land in some new place? Mother, mother, what shall I do?"

"Perseus, listen . . ."

"I am framed for great deeds! I know I am. And now the king knows it too. . . . But glory, glory, glory, what shall I do?"

"Nothing, yet."

"What!!"

"You must grow up first. Become a man before you become a hero. You're only a boy."

"Oh, mother . . ."

"Perseus, the king is not our friend. His one desire is to separate us so that he can force me to marry him. That's why he wants to send you out before you're ripe for combat. But I won't let him."

"Mother, please. . . . You have been my defender long enough. It is time for me to be yours."

"My boy, you have grown beyond me, perhaps. You must ask your father what to do."

"My father? Are you finally going to tell me who he is?"

"Yes, my son, it is time."

And Danae told him what had happened to her in the brass tower. Perseus's eyes grew wider and wider, drinking in the firelight until they became two pools of flame. She had told him before about her imprisonment, but she had never finished the tale.

". . . I was penned up in that stifling prison, pining for light and air, struggling to stay alive. I fastened my eyes to the arrow slit and clung to the sight of the one star I could see. Enlarged

"I am the son of a god," whispered the boy.

by my tears, that star grew until it filled the sky. A blade of light slashed through the blackness and stabbed into my cell. Unlike ordinary light, it didn't spread. The golden blade pulsed, thickened, became a pillar of light, then gathered itself into the form of a man. But taller than any man—with yellow hair and eyes of molten gold, wearing golden armlets and gold sandals, and carrying a jagged shaft of pure light as other men bear spears. I knew he was a god and knelt to him. He raised me gently and spoke in a deep, musical voice: 'Yes, Danae, I am a god. But for the sake of your beauty I have become a man.' "

"Every night he came into my cell as a shower of gold, and he vanished at dawn—just like the evening star."

"Was he my father?"

"He was. And is."

"I am the son of a god," whispered the boy.

"You are."

"What am I then—man, god, or something in between?"

"What you may be, my son, what you may become, cannot be defined by titles, only by deeds. . . . But you are too young to begin, so terribly young! You're the only thing I have now, and I cannot bear to lose you."

"Shall I ask my father if the time has come?"

Danae couldn't speak, she only nodded. Perseus kissed her and rushed out into the windy night.

7

The Dream Tinker

he wind had blown the clouds away, and Perseus prowled the beach under a great chandelier of stars, waiting for dawn. How could so great a day break properly unless he, god–spawned, were there to salute the flaming banners of his cousin, the sun?

It was a sleepless night for the king as well. His brain was a cauldron. "She swallowed the bait," he chuckled to himself. "By this time she has told that accursed son of hers that he is to be king after me . . . when he has returned from a perilous task. Today, he will come to me, asking to be sent on that mission— and I will oblige him, as a kindly patron should. Then I'll turn my attention to his stubborn mother. I'll break her will and possess her beauty. But I have work to do first. I must find a really foul assignment for the lad. What should it be? I need advice from on high. And that means I need a dream tinker."

He clapped his hands; servants came running. He sent them off to find a meadow nymph named Dimona.

In those days it was believed that some unusually talented sorcerers could perform a kind of magic known as dream tinkering. Through certain spells, using certain secret herbs and essences, the tinker unlocked a chamber in the sleeper's mind. In the rich gloom of this chamber, pictures floated, pictures of the future, sent by whatever god or devil manipulated the destiny of that particular person. At this time, an apprentice witch named Dimona was the latest to have impressed the court. She was a long-legged, black-maned filly of a girl with huge, glossy eyes, wild-hearted and fearless as one of the moor ponies, which no one could break. Polydectes disliked her, as he disliked anyone who did not fear him, but he needed her now, and greeted her with a fat bag of gold.

"Keep your money, king," she said. "I can't use it. I live on mushrooms and blackberries and river cress, and dress in leaves, as you see. . . . Lie down and close your eyes and don't open them till I tell you. Take your crown off first. It'll only dig into your scalp."

The king's eyes wanted to fly open, but he pressed them shut. A heavy incense hung on the air, and he knew that Dimona was throwing herbs on a fire. He heard her crooning. The words were muddled so he couldn't understand them, but

It was believed that some unusually talented sorcerers could perform a kind of magic.

the tune was a sleepy one. The sound became a silver river cutting through blackness, and he was afloat upon it, drifting, drifting . . .

Bending over the king, the nymph lifted an eyelid, and saw that he was sleeping deeply enough for her to continue her spell. What she did exactly is a secret that has not come down to us. But she opened a chamber in the sleeping king's mind, revealing a gallery of hideous portraits.

In the dream, Polydectes was himself an invisible presence. A witness. A swift traveler. He swung between sea and land and blue steeps of air . . . and saw things, huge fanged things that swam and crawled and flew. He saw the three-headed dog Cerberus, guarding the tall black gates of Hades. It was snarling, slavering, one mouth chewing a bitten-off hand.

The king traveled up from Hades, up, up—floating on golden air above a blue sea. What was this flying near him? It was something that should not fly, that should not be. Something with horns, with claws, half-lion, half-ram. He recognized it from nursery tales; it was the Chimera. He was seeing it as he slept, but he knew that somewhere it dwelt beyond his dream.

Something else loomed between the king and the sun. It had the body of a tiger, the face of a woman, a serpent's tail, and eagle wings. From one clawed foot dangled a horse, from the other its rider. She screamed at him as she swept past. Or was she laughing? Her laughter was worse. It was the Sphinx.

A down-draft forced him toward the sea. He hovered above a channel. What he saw was the worst navigational hazard in the entire world. Upon one side, a great, gross, bladderlike creature squatted on the sea bottom, swallowing ships and spitting timbers. This was Charybdis, he knew.

On the other side of the channel dwelt Scylla. Her upper body was that of a beautiful sea nymph, but from the waist down she was six ravening wolves. A ship passed close to her. The wolf heads swept the deck, seized six sailors, and ate them alive.

The sleeping king swung above the desert now. It was

Something with horns, with claws, half lion, half ram.
He recognized it from nursery tales; it was the Chimera.

parched, sweltering. He saw a crack in the earth, a drying riverbed with a little muddy wetness left at the bottom. Something huge was slouching down to drink. The Nemean Lion, larger than an elephant, yellow as daffodils, stared with eyes of pure green murder. It roared; the desert shook.

Another riverbank, this one cutting through lush meadows. Along the shore was crawling something too dreadful even for a nightmare. It looked like a riverbed full of crocodiles tied at the waist. The king knew he was looking upon that fabled monster known as the hundred-headed Hydra, which had devoured several generations of heroes. One of them was fighting the Hydra now. An arm flashed, a sword cut off one of the heads. But on the nodding stalk of its neck two new heads grew. And many heads were closing their jaws upon the warrior.

The dreamer drifted again, happy that he saw no pictures—hoping that the parade of monsters had ended. But a paleness was blooming in the darkness. A head grew bigger and bigger as it came toward him. The face was beautiful, but the hair was snakes—writhing and hissing, darting their tongues. It was Medusa. He awoke screaming.

8

The Pledge

ext morning the king greeted Perseus on the steps of the palace. Polydectes was a born actor and knew that he cut an impressive figure, standing a step above the boy against a background of marble pillars, disposing himself so that his purple robe was sculpted by the wind.

He listened gravely as Perseus blurted out his thanks, then laid a fatherly hand on the boy's shoulder. "I know that you want to hear about the task that will qualify you for kingship," he said. "I could assign you one, but I prefer that you name your own. There are many glorious deeds waiting to be done. Among them, killing one of the monsters that plague mankind is perhaps of the highest merit. If you crave such adventure, I might cite several: those dread flying beasts, the Sphinx and the Chimera; Cerberus, the three-headed dog who guards the portals of the Underworld and does not allow the living to enter or the dead to escape; the hundred-headed Hydra, whose heads no foe can diminish as two grow in the place of every one cut off. There are also those sea monsters, Scylla and Charybdis, who drink the tides and devour sailors; the Sirens; the spear-birds of the marsh; and many, many more. I hesitate to even name the worst one, Medusa, because no warrior, however brave and skillful, should go against her. Her aspect is so dreadful that anyone who looks upon her is turned to stone."

"I choose her!" cried Perseus. "I choose Medusa!"

By this time a crowd of courtiers had gathered before the palace. They laughed loudly when they heard the lad's words.

"By the gods," he cried, "who laughs at me will taste my blade before the Gorgon does."

"What blade?" said one gorgeously dressed young man. "I see no sword, and doubt that you own one. Or do you mean that butcher knife of your mother's stuck in your belt?"

"Who will lend me a sword?" shouted Perseus, wild with anger. "I promise to wipe the blood off before I return it."

"Softly . . . softly," said the king. "I'll have no squabbling in my presence. Perseus is my heir now, everyone take note. Carried away by visions of glory, he has made a foolish boast, perhaps, but he is very young. I give him this chance to retract his vow and choose a mission less perilous."

"Thank you, king," said Perseus. "But I retract nothing. I shall return with the head of Medusa or not at all. This is a pledge of blood, Polydectes."

He rushed away from the palace, followed by laughter.

Running across a field toward his mother's house, he met a tall, black-haired girl clad in leaves. She stood in his path. "Stop!" she said.

"I should like to make your acquaintance," said Perseus. "But I must bid farewell to my mother. I leave on the morning tide."

"To seek the head of Medusa, no doubt."

"How do you know?" cried Perseus. "You weren't there when I spoke of this."

"But I know things," said the girl.

"Are you perhaps the young sorceress so popular at court?"

"In all modesty, I am adept at the dark arts . . .
I'm a meadow nymph of the mushroom clan."

"I am Dimona, yes. Everyone thinks I'm an apprentice witch, who learns faster than she's taught. And, in all modesty, I am adept at the dark arts. However, I must confess I've had a headstart. I'm not really human, you see. I'm a meadow nymph of the mushroom clan. I serve the goddess Athena and have been sent here on a special mission to help a half brother of hers who has fallen into deadly peril."

"Half brother? Who might that be?" asked Perseus.

"Athena is a daughter of Zeus. Her half brother would therefore be a son of Zeus. Now the king of the gods has a thousand and three sons at the latest count, but not so many on this small island. In fact, you're the only one."

"Oh . . . you're talking about me!"

"I don't know. . . . Athena said half brother, not half-*witted* brother. With such exalted parentage, your perceptions should be a bit quicker. Of course I'm talking about you. You're the only son of Zeus on this island, and the only one in deadly peril."

"What peril?"

"Is not the king sending you after the head of Medusa?"

"He didn't send me. I volunteered."

"I see."

"In fact, he tried to discourage me. Urged me to do something a little less dangerous. But I chose this task."

"Well, whether he's sending you or you're sending yourself, you're still going—which signifies deadly peril. Do you not agree? Or perhaps you think hunting Medusa is a recreational activity?"

Perseus laughed.

"What are you laughing at?"

"I'm not laughing *at* anything. I'm laughing with pleasure. You're quite beautiful, and you say funny things. Funny, sharp things."

"Oh Goddess, give me strength," cried Dimona. "This is a sweet boy, but with no more brains than a sand crab. Look, Perseus. My mistress, Athena, your half sister, takes a special interest in you and has sent me to help you. But you have to help me help you. So listen carefully, and try to understand. I'll speak slowly."

He laughed again.

"Stop cackling, and listen. How do you intend to journey to the far place where Medusa dwells?"

"The king has offered me a ship," said Perseus. "Complete with crew."

"Set foot aboard that ship and your mission ends right there."

"What do you mean?"

"I mean that the king doesn't plan to wait for you to be turned to stone by Medusa. He expects to hear news of your death within hours of your departure. Every member of that crew is a trained assassin who has been offered a generous bonus to plunge a knife into your heart. So your first instruction from Athena is: Do not board that ship."

"What then shall I use for transport?"

"Look here."

She stooped and lifted a rock. Under it was a pit; in the pit were various objects wrapped in oiled leather. She took up the smallest packet and unwrapped it, disclosing a pair of winged sandals. "These are called *talaria*," she said. "Ankle-wings. Athena is not only a potent weaver, but she cobbles magically too. These sandals are exactly like those she made for another half brother, the messenger god, Hermes. They allow him to fly through the air more swiftly than any bird. They will do the same for you. And you will be the first mortal ever to wear them."

Perseus tried to thank her, but his throat was choked with tears. He had wanted to fly so badly that he had risked his life many times diving off the highest cliffs he could find just to have a brief sensation of flight.

Dimona peeled a larger object of its oiled leather and raised it with a flourish. It was a bronze shield, its center panel so highly polished that Perseus could not look at it, for it held the sun like a mirror.

"This has a double purpose," said Dimona. "When fighting an ordinary enemy, you can flash the sun in his eyes, impairing his vision. But it is specially contrived for hunting Medusa. Because no one can look upon her without turning to stone, you must look only upon her image as reflected in the mirror of your shield."

"Thank you," he muttered.

"Finally—your weapon."

She drew out a sword. Its blade was curved like the new moon; it glittered like a new moon, and was sharper than any blade made by mortal man. Dimona pulled a hair from her head, tossed it up, and as it floated down, swung the sword, cutting the hair in two.

"Here," she said, handing him the weapon. "Strike right and you'll cut through any neck, no matter how monstrous."

"Speak on, sweet tutor," said Perseus. "Instruct me. How do I find Medusa?"

"Her dwelling place is a secret known only to the Apple Nymphs."

"How do I find them?"

"They tend the Garden of the Hesperides, where are buried many secrets, many treasures; among them are two more things you will need to vanquish Medusa."

"How do I find this garden?"

"Ah, my young friend, that too is a secret, known only to the Gray Ones, three weird hags who are sisters of the Gorgons. They dwell on an ice floe, which you will find by flying due north until you feel your marrow freezing. Farewell now, brave lad. Good hunting to you."

Swiftly she brushed her lips over his, wrapping him in a fragrance of crushed grass. He reached for her, but she had vanished.

"I'll come back for you!" he shouted. "And you shan't escape me again!"

He strapped on the sandals and rose straight in the air, shouting with joy. Turning, he swooped down to pick up his sword and shield. Keeping the afternoon sun on his left, he sped over the central mountains of Seriphus toward its northern shore and out to sea, so drunk with happiness that he quite forgot that he, who had never spent a night away from his mother, was now leaving her, perhaps forever, without saying good-bye.

9

The Gray Ones

ow Perseus was flying over gray-black water, littered with ice floes. The air was so cold that it hurt him to breathe. A hailstorm spat ice at him, cutting his face. The cuts bled; the blood froze. He wrapped himself tightly in his cloak, lowered his head, and butted through the freezing wind.

Perseus spotted something below him and flew lower. Three hags sat in a circle on the floe, screaming as they passed things from one to the other. He swooped down and landed silently among them. They stood clad only in their own gray hair, which was so long it dragged on the ice. Their skin was as tough and wrinkled as a crocodile's. Their feet were leather claws. They kept snatching something from one another and screaming softly. Perseus saw that they had a single eye and a single tooth to serve the three of them, and these were what they passed from hand to hand, screeching all the while.

Two of the crones were exchanging tooth and eye while the third yelped angrily, "My turn . . . my turn . . ." Perseus stepped among them, snatched tooth and eye, and stepped quickly back. Immediately the hags screamed, "Where is it? Where's the

*They kept snatching something
from one another and screaming softly.*

eye?" "I gave it to you; you took it. Where's my tooth?" "You took the tooth." "Liar." "Liar." "You're both liars! Selfish, rotten liars! It's my turn for the tooth, my turn for the eye. Give them to me! . . . Give them to me!"

Shrieking with rage, they flung themselves upon one another—slapping, kicking, gouging. They tried to bite, but had no teeth. But their jaws were powerful, their gums tough, and these toothless bites left great bruises. They made so ugly a spectacle that Perseus could hardly bear to look at them. But he could not afford to be squeamish until his task was done.

"Silence!" he roared.

They stopped screaming and turned blindly this way and that. Then they pointed their faces straight at him, and he realized they had developed noses keen as hunting dogs.

"A man!" shrieked one. "I smell a man. A young one."

"A man . . . give me the eye; I want to see him."

"Give me the tooth so that I may smile."

"Listen to me," said Perseus. "I have your tooth and eye, right in my hand. And you shall not have them back until you tell me where the Apple Nymphs dwell."

"The Apple Nymphs!"

"Oh, no, not the Apple Nymphs! Not that secret," yelped one hag.

"It's a terrible secret, a Gorgon secret," cried another.

"They'll tear us to pieces if we tell," said the third.

"I'm hungry now," said Perseus. "I'm about to chop a hole in the ice and go fishing. I'll use this eye for bait. As for this sharp yellow tooth, I can use it also."

He began to chip ice with the tooth, and the crones felt the painful cold in their gums. He pressed the jellied eye lightly between thumb and forefinger, and they felt the pain in their empty sockets. They wept. It was too cold for weeping. Their tears froze and fell musically on the floe.

Swiftly then, gasping and tittering and sobbing, they told him what he had come to find out—that the Apple Nymphs guarded the Garden of the Hesperides, where Hera's golden apples grew and where other treasures and secrets were buried. They also told him of the many brave voyagers who had visited that place, not one of whom had ever come back.

Perseus thanked the Gray Ones, returned tooth and eye, and leaped into the air. The hags' joyful cackling faded on the wind, which grew more and more bitter the higher he flew.

10

The Apple Nymphs

Perseus flew westward. The frozen sea melted beneath him, and became blue water. This gave way to rocky shore, then to a great forest belt, stretching to the horizon. Another sea appeared, then islands rich with meadow and orchard. Dominating the outermost island was a mountain, rearing stark against the sunset.

"Well," he said to himself. "If the hags weren't lying, and I have flown straight, this should be the Garden of the Hesperides."

He dipped toward the earth. Three nymphs were dancing among the apple trees. They were enchantingly beautiful. When his shadow fell upon them, they stopped.

"It's Hermes!" they cried.

"Welcome, sweet Herald!"

"Come down quickly. We're pining for company."

Perseus flew lower and hovered above their heads.

"It's not Hermes!"

"Not a god."

"Much smaller."

"But big enough. Clean and sweet and young."

"Come down!"

"Then what?" asked Perseus.

"You shall dance with us all the sunny day, then dance the night away."

"How do I find Medusa?"

"That's a deep and dismal secret. It will cost you a few kisses and much dancing."

"You're three to one, my lovelies. And I have journeyed far."

"Oh, do stop hovering. Come down or fly away; don't just float there out of reach."

"I can't stop now," he said. "I'm on a mission."

"You men and your stupid missions. When will you learn what women have always known—that happiness is the only victory and love the only happiness? Stay with us, lad, we'll teach you love."

"I'll come back after I kill Medusa. 1 promise. And I keep my promises."

"You may have another mission you don't know about. It has been foretold that a strange young cousin would come to us on wings and change our lives. Aren't you he? Who are you?"

"More than I was and less than I will be," said Perseus. "My father is Zeus, who courted my mother as a sun ray, lancing through her prison wall, illuminating her sorrow, warming her solitude, and leaving her with what turned out to be me."

"If you are a son of Zeus, you are the cousin destined to aid us. Were you sent to us, sweet one?"

"In a sense."

"Oh joy! Then you are he who will free us from the awful vigil of our father."

"Who's your father?"

"See him there on the horizon?"

"That mountain?"

"That's no mountain; that's a Titan—the mightiest of all. What looks like snowy peaks are his hair and beard."

"Why does he hold his arms so broad and wide?"

"He is the Titan Atlas, who rebelled against the gods, and has been condemned to bear this corner of the sky upon his shoulders. But we, his daughters, are condemned, too, living as we do under his stern gaze. And when we're lucky enough to have a guest, why then this father of ours simply stamps his great foot, squashing the visitor like a bug. Won't you please come down?"

"And get squashed?"

"He doesn't know you're here. Storm clouds abet us, lovely boy. They veil his eyes so he cannot see."

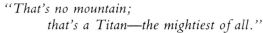

*"That's no mountain;
        that's a Titan—the mightiest of all."*

The Helmet of Darkness . . .
lent invisibility to its wearer.

"Oh nymphs," said Perseus. "Even at this distance I am bewildered by your beauty. I grow dizzy on your fragrance. If I come down and touch your petal skin and breathe your cider breath, I'll go drunk as a bee among apple blossoms. I'll lose my sting, forget my oath, forfeit my newfound manhood, and be no good for you or anyone else."

"What can we do for you, then?"

"Help me, sweet nymphs, and by the gods I'll love you forever. I'll come back with Medusa's head, and tell you the tale of my battle, and dance with you and do your pleasure."

"Let us tell him what he needs to know," cried one nymph. "The sooner he goes, the sooner he'll be back."

The nymphs leaped up and seized Perseus's ankles, pulling him to earth. They clung to him, kissing him and whispering.

He felt his wits spinning, his will melting under their apple fragrance and the touch of their hands and lips. But they were not trying to keep him now—only to be near him, because they could tell nothing to anyone they could not touch. Whispering and murmuring, they told him where Medusa dwelt and how to get there.

Then they pulled him over to a great oak and dug among its roots. Buried there were what looked like a golden bowl and a leather pouch. The bowl, they told him, was a helmet, a most ancient and magical one—the Helmet of Darkness, which lent invisibility to its wearer.

"The pouch is magical too," said one nymph. "It's called the *kibesis*, and it is made from the hide of the Delphic serpent slain by your half brother Apollo at the dawn of time. Only this pouch can contain the head of Medusa, for the envenomed slaver of its snakes will burn through any other. Both helmet and pouch are necessary for your mission. Thank us nicely now."

Perseus put on the Helmet of Darkness and immediately disappeared. They had to grope about to kiss him farewell.

Radiant with happiness, Perseus rose into the air, shouting, "Thank you, beautiful cousins! I shall return!" And he flew swiftly away.

11

The Gorgons

ills flattened as Perseus flew the route given him by the Apple Nymphs. Fields and orchards gave way to a wide, dark plain cut by weed-choked rivers. This was the Land Beyond, called Hyperboreas, meaning behind the North Wind. It was neither earth nor sea but something less than both, a foul marshland from which animals departed, and where no travelers came. Here, Perseus had been told, was where the Gorgons dwelt—snake-haired Medusa and the two monstrous, brass-winged sisters who had followed her into exile. These winged Gorgons were meat-eaters and would snatch any living thing, tear it to pieces in midair, and stuff the gobbets of raw flesh into their mouths.

Perseus had hung the Helmet of Darkness from his belt and was flying bare-headed. For when he wore the helmet he became invisible to himself, and it made him uneasy not to see his own body. He knew, though, that he was getting close to his enemy now, and he decided to put on the helmet. But he had waited too long.

There was a clatter of brass, and he saw two huge shapes rising to meet him, wings and claws gleaming in the muddy light. He was about to clap the helmet on his head when he was

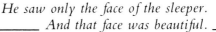

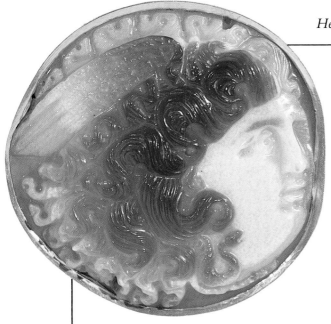

struck by a bold idea. He held the helmet in his hand, hovering, letting the Gorgons see him. He watched them climbing, rise toward him, then separate to attack from both sides.

Exerting his will like a single muscle, he bade his throbbing heart to slow its beat, willed the hot, choking excitement mounting in his chest to turn to an icy calm. He made himself wait until he could see the Gorgons' faces, their bulging red eyes, squashed noses, and yellow fangs, waited until their carrion breath wrapped him in its fumes. Then he put the helmet on his head.

They were about to seize him in their claws. But he had vanished. They groped the thin air, searching, screaming, getting into each other's way, and entangling their wings. They could not find him. They never guessed he was floating directly above them.

Deliberately, Perseus raised his sword and slashed down with all his strength, shearing off the Gorgon's four wings, one by one, listening to the music of his enemies shrieking. They dropped like rocks out of the sky and smashed to the earth. Hearing the sickening sound when they hit, he knew that they were two bags of broken bones and that he could safely descend.

Alighting, Perseus waded through the stinking pools and slogged through the mud until he came to a kind of stone orchard that resembled a graveyard. He realized that he was in a grove of statues. Peering more closely at them in the fading light, he saw that they were the stone figures of men and beasts, the human faces wearing expressions of horror, the animals frozen in mid-flight or cowering in fear. He knew that he was among those who had looked upon Medusa.

Perseus raised his bright sickle sword and covered himself with his shield, judging his movement only by weight since he was invisible to himself. Very carefully, he wove his way through the statues until he heard a sound. Something was breathing heavily, snoring. He saw a glimmer of paleness, a movement. He tilted his shield so that whatever was there would be reflected in the polished metal.

Perseus whipped the blade downward
in a savage backhanded blow.

*Perseus sprang into the air
and flew off as fast as he could.*

He saw a head, saw its hair stand up and writhe, and knew that he had found Medusa. He felt his own hair prickle with horror, as if it too were turning into snakes. He stepped closer, raising his sword.

But the angle of the shield had changed, framing out the snakes, so that he saw only the face of the sleeper. And that face was beautiful. So beautiful and sad that he couldn't bear the thought of striking it from its body. The sword trembled in his hand; the shield almost slipped from his grasp.

He steadied himself—now the reflection had shifted again. He saw the snakes writhing, swelling with fury, biting one another so that the blood ran over Medusa's forehead. And the snake blood reeked of death. He felt himself beginning to swoon in the terrible stench and knew that he must act.

Perseus gripped his sword and felt it fuse to his hand, felt the blade become an extension of his arm, growing white-hot with his own intention. He whipped the blade downward in a savage backhanded blow, slashing down, slashing through snake and tendon, bone and sinew—watching the reflection of her head as it separated from her stalk of neck and rolled off his shield.

Perseus stooped swiftly, lifted the head by its limp snakes, stuffed it into his pouch, and stood gaping in wonder. Where the blood had fallen on the ground, two creatures had sprung forth— a warrior holding his own golden sword and a magnificant white stallion with golden mane and golden hooves and golden wings shaped like those of an eagle. They were Chrysaeor and Pegasus. Their seed had been planted by Poseidon, but Medusa had been unable to bear children while living as a monster, and they had grown inside her womb.

The warrior vanished into the mist. The white horse arched his neck, snorted triumphantly, and pawed the ground with his hoof.

Perseus sprang into the air and flew off as fast as he could. He didn't want to think about the warrior and the horse and where they had come from. He didn't want to think about the head in his pouch. But it was there.

12

Fruit of Victory

Perseus now had two more promises to keep. One offered pleasure, the other vengeance. When confronted by a choice, he preferred to do the harder thing first. But cutting off Medusa's head had horrified him. For the first time in his young life he felt the kind of grief that becomes fatigue. And he decided to visit the Apple Nymphs first and restore himself through pleasure.

They greeted him with joyous laughter, welcoming him as nymphs have always welcomed heroes. They drew him into a wild dance among the apple trees, passing him from one to the other. The dance grew wilder and wilder until it slowed into a fragrant sleep.

Perseus awoke to new pleasures. The blood sang in his veins. The nymphs were as fresh as apple blossoms; they twined about him, urging him to stay.

"I have still another mission before me," he said. "My mother is pursued by an evil king and has no one to help her except me. After I straighten out her affairs, I'll be my own man again."

"Will you come to us again and dance all the sunny day, then dance the night away? Will you . . . will you? Say you will."

"I will!" cried Perseus. "Nothing will keep me away. I'll come back every midsummer and dance with you until the leaves flame. We'll dánce the apples off the trees, press the fruit, and drink the juice. Farewell . . . farewell. . . ."

He picked up the pouch that bore the head of Medusa, leaped into the air, and flew away.

But he should have started his flight a bit sooner. For now the sky was growling with thunder. The mist that had veiled the eyes of Atlas had blown away in the morning wind. And the ill-natured Titan was eager to punish daughters and destroy guests.

"Will you come to us again and dance
all the sunny day, then dance the night away?"

Atlas stamped his foot. The earth shook. He shrugged his shoulders, and comets fell. They fell into the orchard, setting fire to the apple trees. Perseus felt his blood boiling as he watched the trees burn.

He flew straight toward the Titan. Hanging in the air before the giant scowling face, he opened his pouch and pulled out Medusa's head.

"I return good for evil," he cried. "You who do a mountain's task shall have a mountain's form and a mountain's immunity to pain."

He thrust Medusa's head toward the giant eyes. The Titan turned to stone. He became a mountain holding up the western edge of the sky. And he remains Mount Atlas to this day.

Perseus shouted to the nymphs: "You are free now! You may entertain what guests you like—and tread night into day under your dancing feet. And I'll come back as soon as I can."

He wheeled in the air and headed east and south toward Seriphus.

13

The Princess of Joppa

lying home, Perseus was blown off course. The wind carried him to the eastern rim of the Middle Sea, which was the Phoenician shore. He had climbed high; people crowding the shore below looked like an ant swarm. Swooping down, he saw that an enormous mob stood on the beach, staring out to sea. Among them stood a man and a woman wearing crowns.

Perseus looked to where all the people were staring and saw a strange sight. A naked girl was chained to a rock. She was festooned with jewelry, as if about to be married; but her face was a mask of terror. Perseus understood her fear. Plowing toward her was the great blunt head of a sea monster.

Perseus dropped to the beach and spoke to the man wearing the crown: "Who are you? Who is this maiden? Why is she being sacrificed?"

"My name is Cepheus," replied the man. "I am king of Joppa. This lady is my wife, and that unlucky girl is my daughter, Andromeda. But I am not usually asked questions by anyone in that tone of voice."

"And I am not usually treated to the spectacle of a father standing by and watching his daughter being devoured by a sea serpent."

The king swelled with rage. His hand crept toward his dagger. But a thought struck him. This youth had dropped out of the sky, wearing winged sandals. He held a curious antique helmet, a superb shield, and a new-moon sword. Perhaps he was a messenger of the gods and had the right to ask questions. Cepheus fought down his fury and managed a smile.

"I beg your pardon, young sir," he said. "You can understand that a father so distraught would forget the uses of courtesy."

"The beast approaches!" cried Perseus. "Speak quickly!"

"It is sent by Poseidon," said the king. "My wife boasted that she and her daughter were the two most beautiful women in the world, more so by far than any Nereid. And the sea god, who has appointed himself patron of all Nereids, took strong offense. He sent this monster to harry our coast, destroy our ships, and devour our cattle. I consulted an oracle, who told me I could wipe out the insult only by sacrificing my daughter. Needless to say, this causes me great grief. But I am head of state, and must sacrifice my private feelings to public welfare."

"Any state that nourishes itself on innocent blood does not deserve to fare well," declared Perseus. "Poseidon happens to be my uncle; he will forgive me, perhaps, for sporting with one of his pets."

He saw the blunt head coming closer to the rock now and knew they had spoken too long. Not waiting to put on his Helmet of Darkness, he leaped into the air, ankle-wings whirring. He flashed through the air and fell like a lightning bolt onto the great scaly back of the sea monster. The beast arched and bucked, lashing at him with its spiked tail, swerving its head to spit flame. Perseus rode the monster, hacking at the enormous head with his sword. But its scales were polished leather, tougher than bronze; they turned the blade.

Perseus knew there was only one thing to do. He rose into the air, pulled Medusa's head from his pouch, and dived, holding the head before him, dived right at the beast, thrusting the head at it until it almost touched the monster's muzzle.

The beast was caught with jaws agape, spitting fire. And even the flame turned to rosy marble as the heavy statue of a sea serpent sank to the bottom of the sea.

Perseus flew back to the rock, struck off Andromeda's chains, and bore her through the air to where her parents stood.

"Your daughter lives," said Perseus. "I claim her as my bride."

"Your bride!" roared Cepheus. "She is the daughter of a thousand kings, the most richly dowered princess in the East. Do you think I'll give her to a homeless vagabond who's learned a few magic tricks?"

"I see your problem," said Perseus. "If I had let the monster eat her, you could have kept the dowry for yourself. If you weren't about to become my father-in-law, Cepheus, I would tell you how pitiful a king you are, how despicable a father. . . . And if you utter one more syllable I don't like, I shall orphan your richly dowered daughter and make her an even richer heiress. Take care."

He lifted Andromeda in his arms, jewels and all, and flew away, leaving king and queen gaping after him and the harbor half-blocked by the stone serpent.

14

A Hero Comes Home

Perseus flew night and day without stopping, and on the third evening he and Andromeda landed on Seriphus, only to find his mother's house dark and the streets of the town empty.

He hurried to the palace and stood amazed in the courtyard. The marble building was blazing with light and rang with laughter and the clatter of voices. Magnificently clad courtiers thronged the steps and the great hallway. He pushed his way to the throne room.

There he saw his mother. She was dressed in white, hung with jewels, but she was deathly pale and staring glassily. The man clutching her arm and smiling like a crocodile was Polydectes. Perseus realized he had returned just in time, for the king was forcing Danae to marry him, and the ceremony was about to begin.

Perseus heard his own voice thundering through the chamber. "Stop!"

Silence fell. Perseus saw the king staring at him, saw him bare his teeth in a wolfish snarl and nod to his Royal Guard. They raised their axes and advanced in formation.

*"We monsters know that
monstrous destruction leaves no winners."*

"I have redeemed my pledge, oh king," said Perseus. "And I have flown across the world to bring you a gift. But I didn't know it would be a wedding gift."

He put his hand in his pouch. "Mother!" he shouted. "Close your eyes!"

He raised high the head of Medusa, and stood immediately in a gallery full of statues. Stone guards stood with stone axes poised. A snarling statue of Polydectes stood on the steps to the throne. There were statues of courtiers caught in mid-bow, smiling toward the king, or staring toward Perseus. And among the grove of statues stood the white, trembling, beloved figure of his mother.

Perseus went to her and took her in his arms. "I'm home now," he said. "Your past is a nightmare. Your future will be a happy dream. Our enemy, the king, has become his own monument."

"Two kings," whispered Danae. "Praise the gods, Perseus. Their whim is our fate. Look . . ."

She pointed to one of the stone figures. It was a bearded man wearing a crown.

"Who is it?"

"Your grandfather, Acrisius . . . attending the nuptials of

a fellow king, not knowing the bride was his own daughter."

"Your father—who shut you in the tower?"

"Yes, to thwart a prophecy that a son of mine would kill him."

"Delighted to oblige," said Perseus. "My grandfather's stony heart deserves a body to match. I met another loathsome father in my travels. Not quite so bestial as yours, perhaps, but bad enough. That reminds me: I've married his daughter. Come meet her."

The next day, Perseus was polishing his shield, admiring the way the head of Medusa had burned its reflection into the metal. To his amazement, the head spoke out of the shield:

"Throw me into the sea."

He gaped at it silently. It spoke again. "Into the sea, which is my home."

"No! I need you," cried Perseus. "You are the ultimate weapon. With your help, I'll go from victory to victory."

"Beware, Perseus. You cannot be constantly turning your enemies into stone without a deadly hardness entering your own heart. Stop using me as a weapon. Fight in the normal way. Take your chance of being killed. Don't let success petrify you."

"How can winning harm anyone? Only losers lose."

"Not so. We monsters know that monstrous destruction leaves no winners."

"Must I really give you up then?"

"Yes, my lovely boy. For your own sake, be rid of me. Go on to other warm-blooded conquests."

Perseus took Medusa's head to the shore. He looked directly into her face, unafraid, knowing he would not be turned to stone. For he had learned to love her face. And love drives out fear.

He kissed her lips and dropped the head into the sea. It sank to the bottom. And there it is to this day, rolling with the tides, making coral where it goes.

Acknowledgments

Letter Cap Illustrations by Hrana L. Janto

Opposite page 1, LEVIATHAN, *illustration by Arthur Rackham,* from *Arthur Rackham's Book of Pictures,* published by William Heinemann, London, 1913
   Courtesy of The New York Public Library, Prints Collection

Page 3, CLOSED EYES, *painting by Odilon Redon (1840–1916)*
   Courtesy of the Musée Jeu de Paume, Paris
      Photo: Art Resource, New York

Page 4, TREASURES OF THE SEA, *oil painting by Jacopo del Zucchi (1541–1589/90)*
   Courtesy of The Borghese Gallery, Rome
      Photo: Scala/Art Resource, New York

Page 7, NEPTUNE CALMING THE WAVES, *sculpture by Lambert-Sigisbert Adam (1700–1759)*
   Courtesy of The Louvre, Paris
      Photo: Giraudon/Art Resource, New York

Page 8, GRANDE ATHENA DEL PIREO, *ancient Greek statue*
   Courtesy of The Museum of Archaeology, Pireo
      Photo: Nimatallah/Art Resource, New York

Page 10, FRONT BRICK FROM CAPUA, *Etruscan painting of a Gorgon (6th century B.C.)*
   Courtesy of Scala/Art Resource, New York

Page 14, BIRTH OF VENUS, *painting by Odilon Redon*
   Courtesy of The Petit Palace, Paris
      Photo: Art Resource, New York

Page 17, OLD MAN IN A BOAT, *painting by Odilon Redon*
   Courtesy of Hans R. Hahnloser Collection, Berne
      Photo: Scala/Art Resource, New York

Page 18, IN THE DEPTHS OF THE SEA, *oil painting by Sir Edward Burne-Jones (1833–1898)*
   Courtesy of The Fogg Museum, Harvard University

Page 20, ATHENA GIUSTINIANI, *ancient Greco-Roman sculpture*
    Courtesy of the Museo Chiatamonti, The Vatican
        Photo: Scala/Art Resource, New York

Page 23, GORGON AND HEROES, *oil painting by Aristide Sartorio (1860–1932)*
    Courtesy of the Hamburg Museum
        Photo: Scala/Art Resource, New York

Page 24, GORGON, *Etruscan sculpture (6th century B.C.)*
    Courtesy of the Museo Nazionale, Rome
        Photo: Art Resource, New York

Page 26, PORTRAIT OF UPPERCLASS WOMAN, *Roman wall painting*
    Courtesy of Art Resource, New York

Page 28, YOUNG BOXERS, *ancient fresco from Akrotiri, Thera (ca. 1600 B.C.)*
    Courtesy of The National Museum, Athens
        Photo: Nimatallah/Art Resource, New York

Page 30, FUNERAL BANQUET, *Etruscan tomb painting*
    Courtesy of Scala/Art Resource, New York

Page 33, DANAE, *painting by Titian (1488/89–1576)*
    Courtesy of the Kunsthistorisches Museum, Vienna
        Photo: Kavaler/Art Resource, New York

Page 35, HEAD OF BOY, *Etruscan wall painting*
    Courtesy of Art Resource, New York

Page 36, MAENAD, *wall painting from Pompeii (100 B.C.–100 A.D.)*
    Courtesy of the National Museum, Naples
        Photo: Scala/Art Resource, New York

Page 38, DANCING MAENADS, *Roman relief*
    Courtesy of the Museo delle Terme, Rome
        Photo: Scala/Art Resource, New York

Page 40, CHIMAERA FROM ARREZO, *ancient bronze*
    Courtesy of The Archaeology Museum, Florence
        Photo: Scala/Art Resource, New York

Page 42, MEDUSA, *oil painting by Caravaggio (1569–1609)*
    Courtesy of Scala/Art Resource, New York

Page 45, PRIMAVERA, *wall painting from Stabia (100 B.C.–100 A.D.)*
    Courtesy of The National Museum, Naples
        Photo: Scala/Art Resource, New York

Page 48, MERCURY, *by Giorgio Vasari (1511–1574)*
    Courtesy of The Vecchio Palace, Florence
        Photo: Art Resource, New York

Page 50, ICEBERGS, *oil painting by C. D. Friedrich (1774–1840)*
    Courtesy of Kunsthalle, Hamburg
        Photo: Kavaler/Art Resource, New York

Page 52, DESTINY, *painting by Francisco Goya (1746–1828)*
    Courtesy of the Prado, Madrid
        Photo: Art Resource, New York

Page 54, THREE GRACES, *mural from Pompeii*
    Courtesy of The National Museum, Naples
        Photo: Art Resource, New York

Page 57, COLOSSUS, *by Francisco Goya*
    Courtesy of The Metropolitan Museum of Art, New York (35.72)

Page 58, HELMET, *"Corinthian" type (6th century B.C.)*
    Courtesy of The Metropolitan Museum of Art, New York. Dodge Fund, 1955.
    (55.11.10)

Page 60, GORGON FROM SYRACUSE *(6th century B.C.)*
    Courtesy of The Museum of Archaeology, Syracuse
        Photo: Scala/Art Resource, New York

Page 62, HEAD OF MEDUSA, *Greco-Roman cameo*
    Courtesy of The Archaeology Museum, Florence
        Photo: Art Resource, New York

Page 63, PERSEUS AND MEDUSA, *metope from Selinunte*
    Courtesy of The National Museum, Palermo
        Photo: Scala/Art Resource, New York

Page 64, THE ESCAPE OF PERSEUS, *gouache on canvas by Sir Edward Burne-Jones*
    Courtesy of The Southhampton Art Gallery
        Photo: Bridgeman Art Library/Art Resource, New York

Page 66, THE GARDEN, *portion of fresco from Pompeii*
    Courtesy of the Museo delle Terme, Rome
        Photo: Scala/Art Resource, New York

Page 68, THE THREE GRACES, *painting by Pierre Bonnard (1867–1947)*
    Courtesy of the Musée Jeu de Paume, Paris
        Photo: Giraudon/Art Resource, New York

Page 69, PERSEUS WITH HEAD OF MEDUSA, *bronze statue by Benvenuto Cellini (1500–1571)*
    Courtesy of The Brogi Collection, Florence
        Photo: Alinari/Art Resource, New York

Page 70, PERSEUS AND ANDROMEDA, *oil painting by Giuseppe Cesari (1568–1640)*
    Courtesy of Kunsthistorisches Museum, Vienna
        Photo: Nimatallah/Art Resource, New York

Page 72, PERSEUS FREEING ANDROMEDA, *Greco-Roman sculptural relief*
    Courtesy of The Capitol Museum, Rome
        Photo: Scala/Art Resource, New York

Page 74, ARCHITECTURAL VIEW, *wall painting: Panel II from villa at Boscoreale, Pompeii (1st century B.C.)*
    Courtesy of The Metropolitan Museum of Art, New York. Rogers Fund, 1903
    (03.14.13)

Page 76, HEAD OF MEDUSA, *copy of Greco-Roman original by Antonio Canova (1759–1822)*
    Courtesy of The National Museum, Naples
        Photo: Alinari/Art Resource, New York

BOOKS BY BERNARD EVSLIN

Merchants of Venus
Heroes, Gods and Monsters of the Greek Myths
Greeks Bearing Gifts: The Epics of Achilles and Ulysses
The Dolphin Rider
Gods, Demigods and Demons
The Green Hero
Heraclea
Signs & Wonders: Tales of the Old Testament
Hercules
Jason and the Argonauts